W9-BNN-588

THE QUAKERS

THE QUAKERS

JEAN KINNEY WILLIAMS

A m e r i c a n   R e l i g i o u s   E x p e r i e n c e

Franklin Watts
A Division of Grolier Publishing
New York / London / Hong Kong / Sydney
Danbury, Connecticut

Interior design by Molly Heron
Photographs ©:
American Friends Service Committee: 87 (Donald Elder), 15, 83, 84, 86, 93; Ann D.
Cooper/Friends Journal: cover; Archive Photos: 33; Corbis-Bettmann: 9, 13, 20, 24, 28, 30, 35,
39, 46, 49, 51, 52, 56, 57, 75; David Griscom: 95; Friends Historical Library of Swarthmore
College, Swarthmore, PA.: 10; Friends Journal: 79; Museum of Fine Arts, Boston: 6 (Bequest of
Maxim Karolik); North Wind Picture Archives: 22, 32, 36, 37, 41, 64; Sophia Smith Collection,
Smith College, Northampton, MA: 73; UPI/Corbis-Bettmann: 81.

Library of Congress Cataloging-in-Publication Data

Williams, Jean Kinney.
The Quakers / by Jean Kinney Williams.

p.   cm.—(American religious experience)
Includes bibliographical references and index.
Summary: Examines the history, notable individuals,
beliefs, way of life, and current status of this
longstanding Christian group.

ISBN 0-531-11377-9
1. Society of Friends—Juvenile literature.
2. Quakers—Juvenile literature.
[1. Society of Friends. 2. Quakers.]
I. Title. II. Series. Williams, Jean Kinney.
American religious experience.

BX7731.2.W49   1998
289.6—dc21   97-35133
CIP
AC

CONTENTS

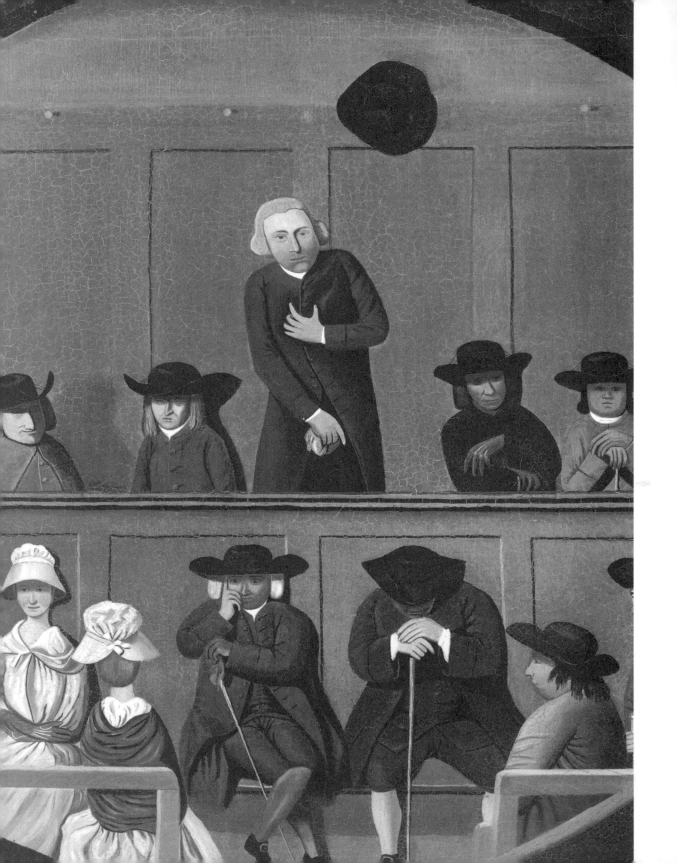

WHO ARE THE QUAKERS?

*T*hree hundred years ago, a new branch of Christianity took England by storm. After enduring a generation of persecution, it emerged as a vibrant social and religious force with more than 100,000 members. Its growth continued as it spread throughout North America. The members of this group gave demonstrations on how to solve conflicts without violence and how to live by the ancient Golden Rule: "do unto others as you would have them do unto you."

Formed in 1648, the Religious Society of Friends of Truth spent its first thirty years challenging England's churches and courts (which usually worked together) to win religious freedom. They took the name of their group from the Christian Bible's Gospel of John, but they got their nickname—the Quakers—because of the physical trembling that came over them during prayer. Although the nickname was first applied in mockery, it gradually became used by Friends, too, until it was no longer considered a negative label.

The man behind the movement was George Fox. As a teenager, Fox felt dissatisfied with the Puritan Church and the Church of England (or Anglican Church), which were the dominant religions throughout England in the 1640s. He left home to find his spiritual place in the world. After a few years of wandering and uncertainty, he found his place one day in prayer.

Fox wanted Christianity to be a direct relationship between each individual and God. He felt sure that all people are endowed with God's "Inward Light" to guide them, if they pay close attention to it. Fox taught that each person must seek God's direction for him or herself and can do so without the aid of trained ministers, sacraments, or even the Bible (though Fox was an avid reader of the Bible and based much of his teaching on it). Fox believed that people could learn to open themselves to the spiritual example of Jesus Christ and experience Christianity at an intensity not reached since the time of the Apostles.

Furthermore, Fox preached, the presence of God in every human makes us all equal, and so he treated all equally. This infuriated his social superiors, such as judges, who expected to be treated *better* than common people. Other ministers were shocked to learn that women were allowed to preach among the Quakers. As a result, Fox and his followers spent much time in dank prisons until 1689, when they won toleration from the English government, which had at first feared that his message would lead to civil and religious chaos throughout the land.

Still, Fox found many eager followers among the common people of England, who were burdened by church tithes (taxes) but felt little appreciated by the clergy. Fox created a different set of terms and customs for his religion. For example, he said churches were

Fox experiences the joy of the inner light.

Quakers gather for worship in simple, undecorated meetinghouses.

unholy "steeplehouses" built by human hands, so his followers met in homes or outdoors at first, and then in simple "meetinghouses." The word "meeting" referred (and still does today) to the worship service as well as to the congregation. Meetings were very simple, with no altar, candles, or music. Sacraments were dropped because they were considered outward, physical forms—such as water in baptism or bread and wine during communion—of the relationship with Jesus that Friends nurtured quietly in their hearts. Marriages were performed without clergy—a couple made their vows to each other during meeting, having already won the approval of other meeting members for their union. Friends, in fact, had no trained clergy. Their ministers were men and women recognized by their meeting as outstanding spiritual leaders. Fox strongly advised his followers to avoid frivolous "time-wasters" such as music, art, and literature.

The Friends traveled throughout England as missionaries, and carried their faith to North America. When Fox died in 1691, the Society of Friends had at least 50,000 members on each side of the Atlantic Ocean.

The Society of Friends had their greatest impact in North America. Though George Fox was the first Friend, perhaps the most famous Quaker was William Penn. Rich, educated, and a sometimes-friend of English royalty (depending on who was on the throne), Penn threw himself into the scandalous Quaker movement head-first. About 20 years younger than Fox, Penn was especially effective as a writer and speaker for the new movement. In the 1680s he combined his business dealings with what he called a "Holy Experiment" by selling thousands of acres of land in North America to European settlers. Pennsylvania became a haven for anyone seeking religious freedom. As Roger Williams had done in Rhode Island, Penn bought land from the Native Americans living in Pennsylvania, and his honesty in those dealings enabled the settlers to live in peace with their Indian neighbors for 70 years.

The Quakers became prominent and prosperous citizens in New England as they gave their beliefs more structure. Though they have never published a "creed," or statement, of their beliefs, their religion gradually grew more rigid. Sometimes they sat through hours and even weeks of silence at meetings as someone awaited word from God's Holy Spirit on what to say, and members were disowned (or lost their meeting membership) for a wide variety of reasons. Their years of public service in the colonies—opening schools and hospitals, settling differences between Native Americans and European settlers, serving as government officials in Pennsylvania and elsewhere—meant little when war fever swept through the colonies during the French and Indian War in the 1750s and during the Revolutionary War twenty years later. The Friends were pacifists, seeking nonviolent solutions to political problems. To the American patriots eager to send the English army home with a fight, that was as good as being traitors.

As they became more and more of a minority in Pennsylvania and suffered for their pacifist beliefs during the Revolutionary War, the Society of Friends withdrew from public life. Although the Holy Experiment had ended, the state government plan Penn had drawn up for Pennsylvania, with its broad range of citizens' rights, influenced the radical new form of government established by the victorious patriots. And though they were no longer dispensing government from state capitol buildings, the Society of Friends still found many ways to influence American society.

The French and Indian War and the American Revolution gave most Friends a chance to exercise their belief that all people—Americans, Indians, or British soldiers—are equally endowed with God's Inward Light, and that killing in war is no different than murder. Also during that century, the institution of slavery, which existed everywhere in the United States, gave Friends another opportunity to demonstrate their belief in each person's basic value.

Quakers were slaveholders throughout colonial America. William Penn simply advised them to treat their slaves kindly. Throughout the 1700s, though, more and more Friends felt less and less comfortable about slavery. Before the end of the next century,

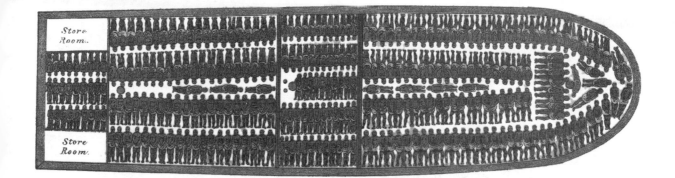

This illustration shows a crowded ship carrying slaves to North America. As the nineteenth century passed, more and more Quakers protested against slavery.

American Friends who still owned slaves had to choose between slaveholding or disownment from their meeting. In the nineteenth century, Friends furthered their stand on equal rights for slaves by helping run various "stations" on the Underground Railroad and operating schools for freed blacks.

While Quakers wrestled with the issue of slavery, other matters were pressing upon them, too. Always striving for self-improvement, eighteenth-century Quaker worship had literally grown increasingly quiet. Other Protestants, both in England and America, were leading movements centered on the Bible and spiritual awakening. City-dwelling Philadelphia Friends did business or had other contacts with those groups. They became influenced by London Friends who were drawn to a more outgoing and zealous branch of Christianity, and they began to accept features of other Protestant religions, such as a paid and trained clergy. However, rural American Friends remained isolated from, and uninterested in, the new ideas. The first split among Quakers came in the 1820s, when some Friends chose to keep their "Quietist" roots while others became more like the evangelical Protestants.

In the meantime, large numbers of southern Quakers left the South—not only to take advantage of land opening up in the Ohio Valley, but to leave the issue of slavery behind. Many Eastern Quakers headed West to claim land, too. As evangelical fervor swept through the western frontier of Ohio and Indiana, Friends were caught up in it, as well. Before the nineteenth century was over, there would be Quakers still practicing the faith much as it originated, as well as those who now hired pastors, sang hymns, and practiced baptism. All called themselves "Friends," but the clashes they had in which they acted like enemies (one group locking the other out of a meetinghouse, for instance) brought embarrassment upon the group that once taught others how to get along.

By the twentieth-century, as two world wars pulled millions of soldiers and civilians into tragic conflict, the Friends began to pull themselves back together. They lobbied for the right to remain non-fighting citizens during World Wars I and II, and they regained their reputation as peacemakers when the American Friends Service Committee (AFSC) traveled around the world to lend aid to countries devastated by war or famine. In 1947, the AFSC was awarded the Nobel Peace Prize. Quaker groups that had been out of contact with each other for decades began meeting again to rediscover their common traits and focus less on their differences.

Today, four main bodies of Friends meet in the United States. You can attend a Quaker meeting where participants, seated facing each other, sit in silence except for the moments when someone is inspired to speak by God's spirit. Those are "unprogrammed" meet-

*In the twentieth century, diverse Quaker groups united in
the common cause of service to humanity.*

ings. "Programmed" meetings may be much like other Protestant church services—led by a paid pastor who gives a sermon, for example—and which might even call itself a Friends church. Even programmed meetings vary greatly from one another. About 70 percent of Friends worldwide attend programmed meetings.

Friends can be found all over the globe; one of the largest groups is in east Africa, where in the early 1900s a few Quaker missionaries from a Cleveland Bible School began teaching about their faith. Today, one of several yearly meetings (an annual meeting pulling in members from several monthly meetings) in Africa may list more than 28,000 members. Africa has the largest number of Quakers—around 120,000.

Altogether, around the world, there are about 300,000 Friends, of which almost 100,000 live in the United States and Canada. Yearly meetings like those in North Carolina, Indiana, Philadelphia, and Oregon claim thousands of members each. Another yearly meeting, in Alaska, listed twenty-seven members a few years ago. It would be difficult to find a religious group with more diversity in culture *and* beliefs than the Friends.

GEORGE FOX AND QUAKER ORIGINS IN ENGLAND

2

*I*n the 1600s, England was a confusing jumble of religion and politics. In the century before, King Henry VIII broke with the Roman Catholic Church because its leader, the pope, wouldn't allow him to divorce his wife (he ended up having six wives, altogether!). Henry established the Church of England, or Anglican Church, in place of Roman Catholicism.

However, King Henry wasn't the first to leave the Catholic church. It had been the only Christian church in Europe until 1517, when a German priest, Martin Luther, rebelled and became the first "Protestant." By the next century, many Protestant movements sprang up throughout England and Europe, each trying to reform the churches that had tried to reform Catholicism.

Religion, politics, and war became intertwined in England in 1642 when civil war broke out, and the religious group known as the Puritans, led by Oliver Cromwell, took over the government. Eventually, the king they deposed, Charles I, was beheaded.

17

Literally wandering through the chaos of that era was George Fox, a young Englishman who was struggling with his own confusion. Born in 1624, Fox came from a hamlet called Fenny Drayton in the "midlands," or middle, of England. He was a spiritual and serious but restless young man who wanted nothing of village life. Trained to be a shoemaker, he also learned to read and he preferred to spend his free time studying the Bible. He had no interest in drinking or gambling, as he saw other young men doing, and his parents' Puritan-influenced church said nothing that seemed relevant to him. He wasn't sure what God had in mind for him, but he didn't expect to find it in Fenny Drayton.

At age 19, Fox left home, avoiding the military conflicts of the time as he wrestled with his inner conflicts: what, he yearned to know, was the truth about God? What did God want George to do with his life? He wandered from town to town, supporting himself as a cobbler and listening to preachers talk about new religious ideas. He heard one preacher speak out against churches supported by the government and argue that people should be free to follow their own callings from God. This idea attracted George Fox—he, too, had little regard for the churches he visited. But that idea could get English men and women in trouble, since all citizens were required to pay the Church of England a tithing—a percentage of their income—whether they attended that church or not.

In his journal, Fox wrote of temptations that hounded him during this period of his life, and he often felt deeply depressed as he made his way to London, a city that teemed with revolutionary ideas about religion. Soon, he added his voice to the clamor, and he began attracting listeners. Churches were only buildings made by men, Fox said, and the established religions led people away from revelations about God, not toward them. That "the Lord would teach his people himself"[1] and speak to individuals was Fox's central theme, and he began winning converts. But he still felt unsure about the path he was to take until finally he was confident he had received a sign from Jesus that he was headed in the right direction.

"There is one, even Jesus Christ, who can speak to your condition," Fox heard one day in prayer. Jesus, Fox believed, was telling him that he, too, had faced temptation, but he overcame it, and Fox could, too. For the first time in years, Fox felt free from the doubts that plagued him, and he began his mission to make religion a personal relationship between God and each individual.

Like many revolutionary religious leaders in history (including Jesus and the twelve Apostles), Fox soon found himself in trouble. His style was confrontational—he would enter churches during worship services and challenge ministers with his ideas. He first was arrested and imprisoned in 1650, charged with blasphemy, or saying something disrespectful to God. But sometimes he took advantage of jail sentences by preaching from his prison window.

He spoke out against tithes, a popular theme with many English Christians, and about the money ministers made from poor congregation members. He told anyone who would listen—he often shouted out his ideas into a crowd when a town held its market— that God would teach them spiritual truth without a minister or an elegant church. The established religious groups in England, such as the Puritans, the Presbyterians, and the Anglican Church, firmly believed that people needed the Bible to understand how to live a

In prison, Fox (left) took strength and comfort through prayer to God.

life pleasing to God. Fox outraged ministers when he claimed that God's Holy Spirit would speak directly to people and guide them. In some ways, though, he outdid the Puritans in sternness. He preached against what he considered to be time-wasting activities such as feasts, wakes, theater, festivals, music, and even star-gazing! Quakers refused to take oaths (such as an oath of allegiance to the king), because it implied that their word was not good without it. In fact, the Quakers' reputation for scrupulous honesty eventually made many of them wealthy in business.

Many people were unsatisfied with the established churches in England in those days, and Fox's message appealed to them. George Fox, who had wandered around England alone for several years, was now the leader of a new religious movement. He and his followers called themselves Children of the Light, and when the group grew to number several dozen, outdoor meetings became a necessity. At one such early meeting, about 200 people sat quietly for almost three hours until someone, moved by the Holy Spirit, finally spoke. Soon, many of them broke into shaking convulsions because, Fox said, "The Spirit is struggling with the flesh."[2] This happened regularly during their meetings, and so outsiders nicknamed them the Quakers.

As Fox urged people to listen quietly for God's spirit to direct them, he spoke out against social injustice. The Puritans taught their members that all people are naturally wicked and needed strong guidance from righteous leaders and that only certain people could hope for eternal life with God. Fox believed the opposite: we are all born with God's goodness or Light within us, and all people are equal, whatever their social status. He angered magistrates by refusing to take off his hat before them: "Does this

trouble thee?" Fox asked a judge, pointing to the hat still on his head.[3] Actually, Fox had just committed two offenses: not only did he keep his hat on, but he addressed the judge as "thee," which was the form of "you" one used with friends or social equals, but not with a social superior.

As much as he sometimes angered church and town leaders, Fox was able to move about fairly freely during this time of government chaos. If he sensed he would soon be arrested, he would try to leave town. He even "convinced" (the term Quakers used for "convert") many of the soldiers stationed in the towns where he spoke. He met with the most success in northern England, and by the 1650s he and other Children of the Light had a large number of converts. His opponents, though, saw him as a lunatic, bursting into churches and shouting his message in town squares.

One woman who heard Fox in her church in northern England and became convinced was Margaret Fell, whose husband was a prominent judge. Their estate, Swarthmoor, became the headquarters of the new movement, which soon numbered in the thousands. Many of the converts were poor shepherds or farmers who felt neglected by the English churches. Much of Northwest England was owned by absentee landlords who cared little for their tenants' struggles. Fox's messages of individual spirituality and social justice appealed to many of them.

Quakers drew the anger of judges by refusing to take off their hats or show proper respect.

The country estate at Swarthmoor became the headquarters for the Quaker movement.

By the mid-1650s, pairs of Quaker men and women were sent out across England with no set agenda, but told only to seek guidance from the Holy Spirit. These missionaries repeated Fox's themes of social equality and the unfairness of tithes as well as authority that depended on social status. The Quaker missionaries kept in touch with the movement's leaders by sending letters to Swarthmoor. One person from that era described an outdoor meeting organized in London with "several thousand" attending, despite the "frost and snow":

John Audland, who very much trembled, stood up, . . . lifted up his voice as a trumpet, and said "I proclaim spiritual warfare with the inhabitants of the earth, who are in separation from God." . . . some fell on the ground, others crying out under the sense of the opening of their [spiritual] states. . . . Oh, the tears, sighs, groans, tremblings and mournings.[4]

The Quaker movement continued to grow as a new English king, Charles II, was crowned in 1660, one year after Cromwell's Commonwealth dissolved. The Children of the Light gathered in plain rooms for meetings that always began with silence as participants awaited God's direction to speak. "They shared their struggles of self-judgment under the Light with other seekers," in addition to sharing "prayers and messages of guidance as well as silence and tears," wrote Quaker historians Hugh Barbour and J. William Frost. They wrote that Fox guided his followers to "Stand still in the Light, and submit to it, and temptations and troubles will be hushed and gone."[5]

But Quaker troubles had barely begun. Although Fox took most of his teachings and spiritual experiences from the Bible, his critics feared mayhem and disorder from a group that listened only to an inner voice that was assumed to belong to God. In London, after Children of the Light arrived there in 1654 and won an increasing number of converts, the established clergy began to campaign against Fox.

As unstable as the government was, it managed to jail Quakers in large numbers for not paying tithes, not carrying proper travel papers, and not swearing an oath denying ties to Roman Catholicism. Hundreds of Friends died in prison. After Cromwell's death, the English government wanted more control over the many religious sects that sprang up during the Civil War years. Though Quakers didn't take sides during that conflict, they were seen as revolutionary, especially as they called for social equality and government protection of the poor and the sick. The uncompromising George Fox even called for giving the churches and homes of the wealthy to the poor.

By 1660, when an army marched through London from Scotland to pave the way for a new English king, the Quakers had "convinced" thousands of converts with effective speaking and well-written pamphlets. They were sending missionaries off throughout Europe and even to the Middle East. They won converts in Ireland and Scotland and in the British West Indies on islands such as Jamaica or Barbados, though missionaries sent to New England were turned away from the Puritan's Massachusetts Bay Colony. In general, converts were most easily made in places where there was a large population of English people. However, they experienced their most difficult struggles in Massachusetts, where English Puritans had fled to create a "pure" society.

The Quakers seldom called themselves Children of the Light after the early 1660s. In the 1650s they had sometimes used the term "Friends" to describe their members, borrowing from a quote by Jesus in the Bible's Gospel of John: "I have called you friends."[6] "Society of Friends of the Truth" was first used to describe the whole sect in 1665, and the term "Friends" is still used today.

The Society of Friends believed they were offering people true Christianity as it was established by the Apostles. George Fox received no payment for his work, but lived off the hospitality and charity of his followers. He married the widowed Margaret Fell in 1669, and there were periods of strife within the Friends movement when Fox encouraged women to participate as speakers or missionaries—a trend that went against Christian and Jewish tradition and made many male Friends uncomfortable.

When converts numbered in the thousands, Fox turned his attention toward the structure of his movement. Worship meetings were established by location and had monthly business meetings; larger quarterly meetings to discuss church business and direction and maintain order were made up of perhaps several monthly worship meetings. Yearly meetings pulled in a large geographic or membership area, such as London Yearly Meeting. The Society of Friends avoided putting their beliefs into writing; to solve problems, they didn't put issues up to vote, but rather would spend much time in prayer until they all arrived at the same "sense of the meeting," or conclusion to a situation. Often, if a problem wasn't resolved that way, it would be set aside and brought up again at another meeting. Fox established schools that were open to all boys and girls; for example, he and William Penn bought land just outside London so that city children "could have a chance to study nature."[7]

In the 1670s, George Fox visited Friends who had moved to the English colonies in America and traveled two years among them, strengthening and enlarging their fledgling meetings. He helped establish the Quaker precedent for friendly relations with Native Americans, treating them as equals and explaining Quaker beliefs. When Fox died in 1691, Europeans, including many Friends, were moving in droves to the new colony of Pennsylvania, founded by the wealthy and influential English Friend, William Penn. There were enough members now within the Society of Friends—at least 100,000

In North America, Fox preached to both Native Americans and European settlers.

in England and America—for more serious arguments over various church issues, but opportunities in Pennsylvania seemed to distract Friends from those problems as they moved on to America. Although they had an established church in England by the time Fox died, Friends never had the influence there they had hoped to achieve. The Society of Friends would make its greatest impact in North America.

PENN'S HOLY EXPERIMENT

*T*he first Quakers in North America were two women who landed in Boston in 1656. Mary Fisher was a young servant who was "convinced" upon hearing George Fox speak in England. Ann Austin, from London, was the mother of five children. Both Austin and Fisher had been sent to the island of Barbados by English authorities for their Quaker activities. From there they went to Boston to plant the "seed," as Friends liked to refer to their faith.

Massachusetts was settled by Puritan pioneers who had left England more than three decades earlier to establish a pure society in North America. The books and papers about the new Quaker faith that Mary Fisher and Ann Austin carried with them threatened the strict religious authority of the Puritans. So the two women, after having their "blasphemous doctrines" burned, were sent to jail.[1] But getting rid of Quakers was no easy matter—as the Puritans soon discovered. While in jail, Fisher and Austin managed to convert a local resident to their faith. That

Quaker preachers were received with hostility in Puritan New England.

man, fined 20 English pounds and banished from Massachusetts, headed for Rhode Island, which had been settled by Anne Hutchinson and enlarged by Roger Williams after they, too, had religious differences with the Puritans. Rhode Island welcomed all religious dissenters, but the Society of Friends wasn't looking for a safe haven. If spreading the seed was dangerous work, then Friends accepted that as part of their faith. Fox himself was in jail in England when he told his followers to "Let all nations hear the word by sound or writing."[2] But the Puritans were not about to give in to a group that allowed women to preach and insisted that all people can be guided by God's spirit without the aid of the Bible, trained ministers, and sacraments, such as baptism, in a formal church.

Fisher and Austin were shipped back to Barbados a few weeks after their arrest in Boston, but another group of Quakers soon arrived. In all, before the end of the 1650s, almost three dozen Quakers tried to penetrate the Puritan stronghold of Massachusetts. The New England Puritans finally enacted the death penalty for Quakers who came back a third time. In the meantime, Quakers on their first or second visits were jailed, beaten, whipped, or had their hands branded with an "H" for heretic. "Great have been the sufferings of Friends in this land," wrote Quaker John Rous to Margaret Fell in 1658.[3] Rous's ears had been cut off by the Puritans for his missionary zeal.

Finally, two Quaker men were hanged in Boston in 1659. The next year, a woman, Mary Dyer, was executed. "Do you think you can restrain those whom you call 'cursed Quakers' from coming among you, by anything you can do to them! . . . The Lord of the

Mary Dyer is led to her execution by Puritan guards.

harvest will send more laborers to gather this seed," Mary Dyer warned her persecutors.[4] The next year, one more Quaker was executed. But then England's royal family, who had no fondness for the Puritans, prohibited them from executing any more Friends, and many were released from jail. The Friends were able to establish meetings in Rhode Island in the late 1650s and win converts (although Roger Williams considered them to be as close-minded about religion as the Puritans!).

Elsewhere in the colonies, the Quakers found that their welcome depended on how strong local churches were. In Virginia, a

Quaker minister was held in a "nasty, stinking prison," where he died.[5] But as Charles II resumed power in England, persecution generally died down, and George Fox and other traveling Quaker ministers, such as Elizabeth Harris, continued to win converts throughout the colonies. Nantucket Island, off Massachusetts, became a strong Quaker community. Colonists who lived away from the main settlements had little government or church authority over them, but many still wanted to live a Christian life. The simple structure of Quaker worship, which didn't require a trained minister, was ideal for those conditions. In Rhode Island, Fox was delighted to

Charles II tolerated, but did not encourage, the Quakers.

33

learn that many important citizens had become "convinced." By the 1670s, the colony had elected a Quaker governor.

The English Quakers defended their faith from Puritan attacks with preaching and writing. In the 1650s alone, they published 540 books and tracts about their faith. By the end of the century, more than 3,700 books and tracts on Quakerism existed,[6] including several dozen written by women. One of the most influential and persuasive Quaker writers was William Penn.

Born in 1644 into the privileged class of English society, William Penn chose the persecuted life of a Quaker to the fury and embarrassment of his father, an admiral in the English navy. Becoming a public speaker and writer for the new religious movement, young Penn was first imprisoned at age 24. While he used his family connections to help other Friends in legal trouble, he seemed to enjoy being a religious rebel. He served more as an important spokesman for the Friends than as a religious leader. He married two heiresses (his first wife died), and one of his business dealings was selling land in what is now New Jersey. Penn lived well, with large estates in England and Ireland, and opened his homes to Quaker meetings and helped finance Quaker activities.

In 1680, Penn appealed to King Charles II for land in America as repayment for money the English government owed his father. By the next year, Penn had a charter from the king for the large territory of Pennsylvania. With that, Penn hoped to further two causes: religious freedom in the form of a "Holy Experiment," and his own livelihood.

Just as he had put his writing skills to work for the Quaker cause, Penn now used his ability to promote land for sale in Pennsylvania. He wrote several pamphlets about the new colony and sent copies to prominent Quakers throughout Great Britain and

Penn stands on the deck of the ship that carried him to North America.

The cover page to one of Penn's pamphlets, which carried news of Pennsylvania to interested people in England.

Holland. Dutch Friends spread his information to other residents in that part of Europe—Penn was looking for any and all buyers, not just Quakers, and he advertised that religious toleration would be extended to all newcomers to Pennsylvania.

He wrote about Pennsylvania's climate and farming conditions—the soil was much better than that of rocky New England—but he neglected to mention the tribes of Native Americans already living there. However, Penn didn't expect to take land from its current inhabitants. Like Roger Williams in

Rhode Island, Penn always approached the Indians with offers to buy land at fair prices, which paved the way for several decades of good relations between the Quakers and Native Americans in that region. By 1682, Penn had sold half a million acres in Pennsylvania. Most of the "First Purchasers" were from England, and less than half were Quakers.[7]

Penn and other settlers arrived in Pennsylvania that same year and slowly built their settlement. Penn founded a city named for "brotherly love"—Philadelphia—which soon had 2,500 residents, 300 homes, and an elementary school. Penn established a Frame of Government for the new colony that guaranteed religious freedom and prohibited the death penalty (used for dozens of infractions in England) except for murder or treason. Penn outlawed gambling and planned to keep peace without a state militia. "Let men be good, and the government cannot be bad," Penn wrote in the Frame.[8]

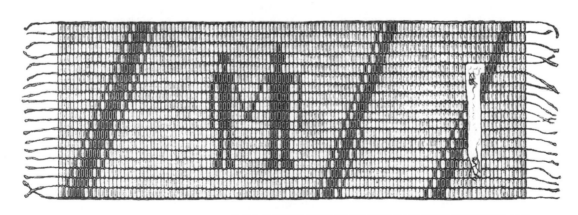

Native Americans made this belt in commemoration of a treaty signed with Penn. It shows a Native American figure (left) shaking hands with a large man wearing a hat—Penn.

The map Penn received with his land charter from the king contained an error, giving Penn land that already belonged to Lord Baltimore in Maryland. Penn returned to England to tend to his sick wife and work out the land-boundary issue. He hoped to return to America within a couple of years, but he ended up being away for sixteen years. The boundary issue between the two colonies was resolved when surveyors marked the current state borders between Maryland and Pennsylvania—the Mason-Dixon Line.

Though a visionary and natural salesman, Penn's business sense was often lacking, and his land sales in Pennsylvania, which he had hoped would solve his financial difficulties, increased his debt. The settlers didn't want to pay him money they had agreed to pay originally, and they expected Penn to support the state government himself. Penn also made some poor choices in hiring men to govern in his absence, and their incompetence increased his financial problems. Before his death in 1718, he would even spend time in debtors' prison, though Friends raised money for his release. So the first settlers of Pennsylvania, still under the strong influence of the Quaker religion, learned about governing themselves through trial and error.

As the early days of Quakerism passed with the deaths of George Fox (in 1691) and other influential leaders, the 100,000-member group of Friends lost their radical momentum as religious toleration made their faith more acceptable. Considered social outcasts in England in the 1660s, Friends now set the standards for society in Philadelphia, which became the government and cultural center of the new colony.

Since they shunned the arts and leisurely pastimes but valued education, Friends began to excel in industrial science in England and in agriculture in America, where Friends supported lending libraries. Their reputation for honesty made many Quaker businesses wealthy.

Within fifty years of its founding, Philadelphia had become one of the largest and most important cities in the colonies.

A majority of members of the Pennsylvania state government were Quakers and belonged to the Quaker Party. The Quaker party, which also had non-Quakers as members, in general stood for lower taxes, religious freedom, and peaceful relations with neighboring Indians.

By the 1700s, the typical Quaker family was respected, successful, and living an austere life with their distinctively plain clothing and speech, however wealthy they were. Like many new religious groups, the Quakers liked to think of themselves as separate and different from the rest of the world. In fact, wealth, or rather the act of flaunting it, became a subject of reform among the Friends. "Visiting" committees were established in various meetings to pay calls on wealthier members and encourage them to live more simply.

Some Friends chose to be disowned by the meeting rather than scale back their lifestyles.

The Quaker religion, though still considered open to direction from the Holy Spirit, became much more regulated, and offenses such as marrying outside the faith or listening to music could cause disownment from the meetings. Regulations about Quaker life were gathered into what were called "Disciplines" and printed. Several times a year, Monthly Meeting members were required to answer a list of "Queries," either in person or in writing, such as: "Are Friends careful to attend Meetings at the time appointed and to refrain from sleeping or chewing tobacco in Meetings?" "Do young Friends keep company for marriage with non-Friends or marry without parental consent?" "Do Friends stay free from music houses, dancing, and gambling?"[9] Parents were expected to be good role models, and Quaker learning was as much about simplicity and moderation as about reading and writing.

Quaker meeting-houses were plain and undecorated. There was no music or hymn-singing, and men and women sat separately on hard benches. One Swedish visitor to a Philadelphia Friends' meeting in 1750 described the worship service he attended:

All Friends sat in silence from 10:00 A.M. until 11:15, when Finally, one of the two . . . old men in the front pew rose, removed his hat, turned hither and yon, and began to speak. . . . In their preaching the Quakers have a peculiar mode of expression, which is half singing, with a strange cadence and accent, and ending each cadence . . . with a half or . . . a full sob.

The Swedish visitor gave an example of the man's preaching, which was typical in Quaker meetings: " 'My friends / put in your mind /

Quaker meetinghouses were plain and simple.

we / do nothing / good of ourselves / without God's / help and assistance / etc.' " The whole sermon, the visitor said, lasted about 30 minutes.[10] Anyone, regardless of gender or social status, could be a minister.

Two issues the Friends faced in early America were slavery and relations with Native Americans. Believing the "Inward Light" of God to be in each person, Friends saw Native Americans and Africans differently than most other white immigrants did. Early records of Quakers in America tell of Friends frequently traveling through Indian territories unarmed and unharmed. "There were several instances when an Indian tribe refused to sign a treaty with white men unless a Quaker was there to witness the deed," wrote Margaret Bacon in her book *The Quiet Rebels*. "The long period of peace with the Indians . . . probably contributed more than any other single factor to the material success of the new colony."

Ironically, William Penn's own children, who were prominent in Pennsylvania affairs but not members of the Society of Friends, contributed to the end of peace between Pennsylvania settlers and their Native American neighbors. Thomas Penn tricked the Minisinks out of land they didn't want to sell. The Minisinks eventually moved west, having become hostile to white settlers. Non-Quaker settlers in west Pennsylvania didn't try to get along with local Indians. Often, proprietors, or land dealers, didn't bother buying land from them before selling it to Europeans. Land agreements made by William Penn were changed or even overturned. By 1754, the French had little trouble convincing the Iroquois to join them in fighting British colonists.

In any case, the Quakers, along with other peace-seeking religious groups such as the Mennonites, continued to serve as intermediaries between native tribes and white government officials. The rights and living conditions of Native Americans remained a strong Quaker concern for many generations.

Friends first came into contact with African slaves when their missionaries traveled to the West Indies, where British-owned sugar plantations used slave labor. When George Fox observed slaves, he advised their owners to educate them, teach them of Christianity, and perhaps free them after a certain number of years. Gradually, slave-owning and importing, and then almost any kind of participation in businesses that used slave labor, became an issue that challenged Friends. By the time the American Revolution ended in 1783, the Quakers had started to withdraw from public and political life in Pennsylvania and Rhode Island. Instead, they increasingly turned their attention toward social concerns that tugged at their Christian consciences. For more than 100 years, perhaps no social issue concerned the Quakers more than slavery.

THE COST OF CONSCIENCE

4

*A*s the Quakers confronted the issue of slavery, they also had to decide how they would react to military conflicts. During England's Civil War in the mid–1600s, Friends remained neutral with little consequence. When they were persecuted, it was for religious reasons, not for refusing to take sides in the war. During the Friends' first seventy years in America, England was at peace, and Friends could exercise their peaceful approach to life among Native Americans with few challenges. The era of peace also allowed Pennsylvania to remain almost militia-free.

But when the French and Indian War erupted in North America in the 1750s, the Quaker-led government of Pennsylvania couldn't convince other residents of the colony to resolve the conflict peacefully. And when the Revolutionary War began in 1775, the Quaker attempts to remain neutral and find peaceful solutions to the war were seen as treason by such patriots as Sam Adams and Thomas Paine. During both wars, Quakers were imprisoned or fined for not

fighting or paying a replacement to fight for them. Friends who were disowned for supporting the Revolutionary War formed the Society of Free Quakers, which included Betsy Ross and war general Nathanael Greene. But that faction died out within about fifty or sixty years.

During the Revolutionary War, more non-Quakers settled in Pennsylvania, ending William Penn's "Holy Experiment." The Society of Friends, as they dealt with the consequences of staying neutral and refusing to pay war taxes, withdrew from public life. The move was actually welcomed by many Friends, who feared that their faith was badly influenced by too much contact and interaction with the world. They sent their children to Quaker boarding schools to lessen the chances of children marrying out of the faith, and they retained their simple clothing and plain speech, much unchanged from one hundred years earlier.

In spite of their withdrawal from the world, the Quakers didn't forget those who were unable to fend for themselves. Quakers in Philadelphia, for example, established the first hospitals for the mentally ill. Due to Quaker influence, Pennsylvania led the way in prison reform. But the most consuming issue for Friends in this era, in addition to war neutrality, became slavery. The first antislavery society in the colonies was formed in 1775 by Friends in Philadelphia.

One eighteenth-century Friend who stands out for his contributions to Quaker life and thought is John Woolman, born in 1719. He left behind a journal, published after his death in 1772, which urged Quakers to see the issue of slavery for what it was—unacceptable. He spent much of his life seeking friendship with and better awareness of African slaves, their owners, and Native Americans.

Woolman was born into a devout Quaker family in New Jersey. He attended Quaker schools and worked as a shopkeeper. His first brush with slavery occurred when his employer asked Woolman to make out a bill of sale, or receipt, for a slave woman who had just been sold. He did, but was stung by the situation. As a Quaker shopkeeper, he quit selling fancy buttons, trimmings, and fabrics, and then he became a tailor to avoid those conflicts altogether and to have the freedom to travel as a minister. He also farmed and even ran a school for a while, keeping classes small so that he could get to know his pupils.

His writings describe a constant awareness of God before whom, he wrote, he was "often bowed in spirit" and he had a variety of holy visions throughout his life.[1] He read about religion by a variety of authors, including those who were Anglican, Moravian, Roman Catholic, and Congregationalist (the church that developed from the Puritans).

Woolman traveled through the South in 1746 and observed slavery firsthand, noting what seemed to be the easy life of slaveholders. Foreshadowing the bloody conflict that was still more than 100 years away, he wrote that he felt "a dark gloominess hanging over the land."[2] After returning home, he wrote about his views, which later were printed and distributed among yearly meetings in 1754. His close friend, Quaker Anthony Benezet, joined him in these antislavery efforts. Benezet helped form the first abolitionist society in America, and he was the first Friend to open a school for black children. He added to the public debate by publishing his research about the "Manner by Which Slave Trading is Carried On." In the 1750s, some Friends still owned slaves. Woolman joined a committee that tried to convince Quaker slave owners in the Philadelphia area to free their slaves. Because slave labor was sometimes involved in producing dyed fabric, Woolman began to wear only undyed clothing.

Woolman and Benezet also were drawn to the situation of Native Americans who had moved aside for incoming white settlers. Woolman visited the Indian territories to learn more about them and discuss his and their spirituality. In one case, he disarmed a ready-to-battle Indian man with his sincere, friendly approach. In the early 1770s he visited England as a minister, traveling in the steerage compartment of the ship with the poorest passengers. While

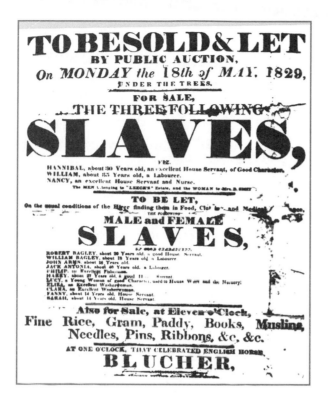

The selling and trading of slaves, as advertised in this poster, drew louder and louder protests from Quaker writers.

in England, he caught smallpox and died in 1772, the same year that his yearly meeting in New Jersey decided to disown any remaining Quaker slaveholders.

When Woolman's journal was published two years later, it inspired a stronger antislavery movement among Friends and other Christians. After the Revolutionary War, Quaker-influenced Rhode Island passed the first law to abolish slavery within its borders, and Quaker influence helped lead both America and England to end slave trading by 1807. Quaker slave-owners in the South were often prevented from freeing their slaves because of state laws, but sometimes they could work around the laws. During one meeting a Pennsylvania Quaker minister named Sarah Harrison convinced Quaker slaveholders to free fifty slaves. Large numbers of Southern Friends began migrating north and west to the slave-free Northwest Territory, hoping to leave the slavery issue behind them—as well as to claim a part of the new lush farmland becoming available to settlers there.

Beginning in the nineteenth century some Quakers began exploring ways to revitalize their faith, which caused changes—and divisions—throughout their Society (which will be discussed more in the next chapter). But antislavery work as well as reaching out to free black Americans was one cause that many Friends could agree upon, though at first it polarized both conservative and liberal, action-minded Friends.

John Greenleaf Whittier was a Massachusetts Quaker poet who became consumed with the abolitionist cause. Although after the Civil War he became quite popular with poems about religious faith and simple Quaker life, he spent thirty years denouncing both southern slave-owners and Northerners who ignored the situation. Through his writing, Whittier helped make slavery a national issue, and he urged conservative Friends to rally to the cause.

Some abolitionists took their cause to the press, literally, by publishing newspapers that condemned slavery. The state of Georgia offered $5,000 for the arrest and conviction of one such publisher, William Lloyd Garrison, whose newspaper the *Liberator* was based in Boston and who was neither arrested nor convicted by his fellow Yankees. Garrison had been influenced by the first abolitionist newspaper, the *Emancipator*, published first by Quaker Elihu Embree in Tennessee and then by another Friend, Benjamin Lundy, who

Quaker abolitionist John Greenleaf Whittier

moved it to Baltimore, Maryland, the heart of America's slave trade. Lundy was lecturing in Boston when he happened to meet Garrison, who joined Lundy's newspaper, *The Genius of Universal Emancipation*.

Later, having moved back to Boston, Garrison began his own abolitionist newspaper. In 1833 he led a Philadelphia meeting where the American Anti-Slavery Society was formed, and looking on (but not invited to participate) was a group of local concerned women. Among them was a 40-year-old Quaker wife and mother, Lucretia Mott, of a prominent Quaker family—the Coffins. She and her hus-

51

band, James, were strong opponents of slavery; James, a merchant, had already given up all sales of cotton, perhaps the biggest product of southern slave labor, though their family income suffered as a result.

Inspired by the Philadelphia meeting, Lucretia formed the Philadelphia Female Anti-Slavery Society, and in 1837 she was instrumental in organizing a national abolitionist society for women. She learned that the abolitionist movement was not important to all northerners and that, though the Friends were accustomed to women speaking in worship meetings, most Americans still were not. Because many abolitionists were women who spoke before

Lucretia Mott organized women's efforts against slavery.

public gatherings, it was an unpopular cause among conservative Friends and non-Friends alike. Lucretia Mott experienced this anti-female attitude during her abolitionist battles, and she went on in the 1840s to address women's rights. That cause and her antislavery work often were not well-received by other Quakers, who feared abolitionism could lead to war. In fact, the abolitionist work of John Brown came to a violent end in a clash with U.S. forces at Harper's Ferry, Virginia, in 1859.

Lucretia Mott came close to being disowned from her meeting for her activism. Conservative Friends were more likely to write their congressmen and lobby against slavery quietly. They bristled at accusations by radical Quaker abolitionists, such as the influential Elias Hicks, that anyone who bought goods made or grown by slave labor was helping the institution of slavery.

PRUDENCE CRANDALL

William Lloyd Garrison's writings in his abolitionist newspaper the *Liberator* inspired a young Quaker woman in Connecticut, Prudence Crandall, to take a stand that took her from her position as a respected school teacher to that of a reviled outcast.

Twenty-eight years old and educated at a Quaker boarding school in her native Rhode Island, Crandall was hired in

1831 to establish a Female Seminary in Canterbury, Connecticut. The school "became an immediate success," wrote Daisy Newman, who tells the story of Prudence Crandall in her book *A Procession of Friends*. Prudence's employers, who were also the parents of the students, considered her a fine teacher of "sterling character." But Crandall's Quaker beliefs in equal treatment for all, encouraged by Garrison's abolitionist newspaper, were soon put to a test.

"Sarah Harris, a local Black girl, came to Prudence and pleaded for an education, so that she might be enabled to teach children of her own race," Newman wrote. Crandall refused at first, knowing it would upset the other girls' parents; many of them belonged to the *American Colonization Society* "which wanted to send the Blacks back to Africa" rather than assimilate former slaves into American society. But a Bible verse about oppression and oppressors was much on Prudence's mind. Not wanting to be an oppressor, she admitted Sarah Harris to the school.

Not only did she then refuse her employers' wishes to discharge Sarah from the school, but "she put an advertisement in the *Liberator* for young ladies of color [as students] and dismissed her white pupils. The Canterbury people were stunned." At a town meeting, local citizens unearthed an old law against "vagrancy," where any nonresident coming through town could be asked to leave or pay a fine—or face a whipping. A Unitarian minister from a nearby town paid the fines of the seventeen black girls who were charged under that law when they arrived to attend school.

The town's next move was to petition the state government to outlaw blacks from other states from attending school in Connecticut. "Known as the Connecticut Black Law, this was passed in April 1833," Newman wrote. Prudence Crandall was arrested and jailed for breaking this new law. Her sister replaced her as teacher, though the school had become a target for "stones and rotten eggs that the neighbors hurled through the windows. . . . The well had been poisoned." Prudence's father brought water from his farm to the pupils and teachers. Her bail was paid by the kind Unitarian minister.

The *Liberator* reported the situation, and it became a national issue. A New York businessman sympathetic to the abolitionist cause, Arthur Tappan, paid for Prudence's lawyers and visited the controversial scene. Appalled by what he witnessed in Canterbury, he put up a printing press in a nearby town to report on what was happening—since local newspapers had failed to do so. Prudence Crandall was convicted during a summer trial; the state supreme court, "unwilling to get involved in such a touchy question, refused on technical grounds to try Prudence." The school building had been burned to the ground and the well filled with manure. Crandall's stay in Canterbury finally came to an end when she married a widowed Baptist minister and moved to Kansas. But she remained in the public mind, and several well-known Americans, including Mark Twain, pressured the Connecticut state legislature to officially renounce what had happened to her in 1833. She was an old woman and widowed when the state finally granted her an annual pension of $400.

*Runaway slaves
arrive at the
Coffins' house.*

An English Friend who made an impact on attitudes toward slavery was Joseph John Gurney. Traveling in America from 1837 to 1841, he visited the Carolinas to get a personal look at slavery, and he compared it to life in some British Caribbean islands, where slavery had been outlawed. He published a letter that he wrote to U.S. Senator Henry Clay about his conclusions: freed blacks lived more stable lives and worked harder for their employers, who made more profits as a result. Gurney predicted that American slave owners would reap the same benefits if they freed their slaves. He then met with politicians in Washington to lobby his point of view.

After the days of George Fox's radical behavior, Friends had become more scrupulous about obeying local laws and finding peaceful ways to create change. But slavery was one issue on which some Friends felt compelled to break the law, such as hiding runaway slaves in the Underground Railroad. However, the more conservative Friends believed that secretly breaking the law was wrong no matter what. "No issues aroused livelier debate within the Society of Friends at this period than . . . participation in the Underground Railroad," wrote Margaret Bacon in her book, *The Quiet Rebels: The Story of the Quakers in America*.[3]

The so-called "president" of the Underground Railroad was Friend Levi Coffin, who had houses in Indiana and Cincinnati, Ohio, near Kentucky, where slavery was legal. Coffin and his wife, Catherine helped an estimated 2,000 slaves escape over a twenty-year period. Coffin wrote that he and his wife "knew not what night or what hour of the night we would be roused from slumber by a gentle rap at the door."[4] He established a store in Cincinnati where he sold cotton and sugar that didn't originate from slave labor, and he raised money to support work programs for freed slaves in Arkansas.

In the last two decades before the Civil War, having realized that quieter protest methods were having little impact on the institution of slavery, the divisions between Friends over slavery began to close. As important as work on the Underground Railroad was to some, or writing about the evils of slavery, others decided to work with freed blacks in both northern and southern states, primarily in education or resettlement programs.

But still other issues divided the Society of Friends. Beginning in the 1820s, just who really was a true Quaker became a question that ripped the fabric of the Society of Friends.

FRIENDS BECOME ENEMIES

5

*I*n the first 100 years of its existence, the Society of Friends went from being a joyous band of religious rebels, drawn from the bottom of England's social ladder, to becoming a large, stable, prosperous and even respectable segment of American and English society. Although he disapproved of their refusal to serve in the American Army during the Revolutionary War, President George Washington declared that "there is no denomination among us who are more exemplary and useful citizens" than the Quakers.[1]

In the decade before the American Revolution, about half of the 50,000 to 60,000 Quakers in America were centered in Philadelphia and Maryland, while others were scattered from Maine to Georgia. They had come a long way from the days of being a tiny minority suffering imprisonment, hangings, and whippings at the hands of Puritans.

As they turned away from public life after the Revolutionary War, Friends began looking inward to strengthen their Quaker identity and purpose. Simple clothing and home furnishings were emphasized, and drinking habits among members were scrutinized. As we've already seen, slaveholding was another fact of eighteenth-century life that Friends worked to change.

As the eighteenth century progressed, the number of misdeeds for which Friends could be disowned from their monthly meeting increased. With the establishment of Quaker schools, and as families often associated only with other Quakers, they "concentrated more and more on inward life . . . turn[ing] their aggression upon themselves," becoming "increasingly strict about plainness," wrote Daisy Newman in *Procession of Friends*.[2]

The traditional label describing Friends' faith was "quietist," because its members waited quietly in individual prayer or in meeting for God's direction in what to say or how to proceed in a matter. Without continuous listening, it was believed, people fell into sin. As a result, all speaking at meetings became suspect—was it God who led a person to speak, or was it their own impulses? And so the silent meetings stayed silent, sometimes for months at a time. It isn't surprising that, for some Friends, revitalizing the Quaker faith became an important issue in that era.

Early Quakers didn't always consider the Bible as important as the "Inward Light" for spiritual guidance. But as the nineteenth century approached, some Quakers wanted to give the Bible a more prominent position in the faith and began forming "Bible Societies" and advocating certain beliefs that must be professed in order to be a true Christian as well as a Friend. Around them, other Protestants, with whom Quaker businesspeople might come into contact, also were advocating Christian beliefs based on the Bible and spent much energy spreading their message, or evangelizing. During the eighteenth and nineteenth centuries, the Quakers influenced the British and Americans in social issues and were among the largest Protestant denominations. Now, the Quakers were greatly outnumbered by Baptists, Presbyterians, and Methodists, and they in turn began to be influenced by the changes in other Protestant groups.

Urban Friends in England and America—groups that had the most contact with other religious groups—inspired a Quaker movement that centered on the Bible and on specific beliefs about Jesus of Nazareth. At the same time, Quakers joined the droves of eastern Americans who headed west to the Ohio River Valley and Great Lakes regions. Some southern Quaker communities were practically deserted when entire monthly meetings of Friends moved north to the new territory. By the 1820s, there were more than 20,000 Friends living in Indiana; within another decade, Friends were settled in Iowa. New yearly meetings were established, and Quaker communities began forming on the American frontier just as they had 150 years earlier along the Atlantic Coast. They established schools, built meetinghouses, and attempted to keep their simple Quaker dress and plain speech.

Among early nineteenth-century Friends, disagreements over what was "Truth" in Quakerism emerged, probably brought on both by the dullness that had crept into their worship as well as by the feverish certainty that evangelical Christians demonstrated in their own beliefs. Just what was the "Inward Light," and what exactly did it have to do with Jesus? How much authority should actually rest with Scripture from the Bible, and did all Friends have to believe the same things about Jesus to be called Friends?

One preview of future disagreements over these issues occurred in London in 1801. Hannah Barnard, a New York Quaker, was in

*In the early nineteenth century, some Quakers began to frown upon
the traditional meeting and the doctrine of the inward light.*

England traveling as a minister. Under questioning from London
Yearly Meeting leaders she admitted that she couldn't consider Old
Testament stories from the Bible as truthful, nor was she certain
whether Jesus had actually been born to a virgin mother, as the
Gospels state. The London meeting declared Barnard unfit to be a
Quaker minister, and she was disowned by her monthly meeting

when she returned home. Those who disagreed with her disownment could choose to leave or be disowned, as well.

In the next several years, both English and American Quakers began to incorporate some examples of evangelical Christianity into traditional Quaker quietism. English Friends began the trend as the older leaders of traditional quietism began to die. Philadelphia and New England Friends often looked to the London Yearly Meeting for leadership. The Philadelphia Yearly Meeting added to its discipline book a new reason for disownment: "to deny the divinity of our Lord and Savior Jesus Christ, the immediate revelation of the Holy Spirit, or the authenticity of the Scriptures."[3] Evangelical Christians claimed that liberal Christians, such as the Unitarians, downplayed the importance of Jesus and the Biblical claims about him; much the same argument was occurring between quietist and evangelical Friends.

The "match" that finally lit the fire came in the person of Elias Hicks, who, as we saw in the last chapter, already was used to fanning the flames around the slavery issue. He was a minister in his Jericho, New York, monthly meeting as well as a husband and the father of eleven children. Though his education had been limited, he was described as having "a rational, probing mind, and as a young man developed a distaste for dogma and a devotion to the search for the truth."[4]

Hicks was in his late 70s when he ignited the first Quaker split in 1827 in Philadelphia. A traveling minister and traditional quietist, Hicks was seen by evangelical-leaning, or "Orthodox," Friends as having incorrect beliefs about Jesus. Hicks resented their attempts to correct him or keep him from speaking at meetings. At the

Philadelphia Yearly Meeting in 1827, Hicks' followers and defenders, who became known as "Hicksites," came to a clash with orthodox Friends over who would serve as clerk of the important annual meeting that year. The two groups, far beyond agreeing on the "sense of the meeting," then separated.

The Philadelphia Yearly Meeting was split in two. It divided individual families and affected schools and meetinghouses operated by what had been one group. In general, the rural Friends remained Hicksites, and the urban Friends joined the Orthodox group. In the Philadelphia Yearly Meeting the Hicksite faction outnumbered the Orthodox more than two to one (about 18,500 to 7,350).[5] Only three monthly meetings became Orthodox, though they had a majority of ministers.

Most Hicksites had a firm belief in Jesus' divinity and in the truth of Scripture, but they wanted to remain focused on the "Inward Light of Christ" to direct their lives, while most Orthodox Quakers wanted to de-emphasize it and have a more definite set of beliefs based on the Bible. The Orthodox claimed that because some Hicksites didn't believe in the divinity of Christ, they were not true Friends, and therefore Quaker property should fall into Orthodox Friends' hands. Not surprisingly, Hicksites suggested property be split according to the size of each group. Each group considered themselves Friends, but not the other. The next year, they held separate Yearly Meetings, and each vied to be recognized by the London Yearly Meeting. London Friends, who had helped sway American Friends toward Orthodoxy, did not communicate with the Hicksites.

The separation was contagious and affected other yearly meetings in various ways. Baltimore, Ohio, and Indiana split into roughly even groups, while New York formed two yearly meetings and was largely Hicksite; North Carolina Friends had so few Hicksites that no split occurred there.

The most un-Friend-ly confrontation between the two factions took place in Mt. Pleasant, Ohio, in 1828, where the situation was stirred up by visiting Orthodox and Hicksite ministers at the Ohio Yearly Meeting. The "Orthodox determined to control the Yearly Meeting by using door keepers who allowed only their partisans to enter the meeting-house. The Hicksite men appeared en masse before the doors and shoved their way inside." Before long, the meeting "disintegrated into a riot," as it's described in *The Quakers*.[6] The Orthodox Friends had the numerical advantage in Ohio (about 10,000 to 6,000), as was true of Yearly Meetings in most of the Midwest. The Bible-oriented evangelical Christian groups that influenced eastern and English Friends had made their way west, too, and found Friends there, far removed from the heart of Quakerdom in Philadelphia, more receptive to their ideas.

Like a great earthquake, the schism between Friends in the 1820s and 1830s had aftershocks. The Orthodox had hoped to avoid further splits by stating a set of firm beliefs, but some Friends within their ranks wanted to preserve at least some links to early Quakerism, with its quiet prayer and acknowledgment of the Inward Light. Once again, a London minister came visiting and set off another round of divisions.

Joseph John Gurney came from a large and prominent English family of Friends. Charming, well-educated, and an effective speaker, he had leaned toward joining the Church of England, as had several of his siblings, but instead decided to try and influence, and perhaps "wake up," Quakerism with an increased evangelical fervor. He arrived in America in 1837 for a three-year visit and when he left, the Orthodox Friends had split again.

There were "Gurneyites," who wanted to turn away from the inner light notion once and for all and spread their message of Jesus as savior much as the other evangelical Protestant groups did. The "Wilburites," a small faction of Orthodox Friends, believed, like their chief spokesman John Wilbur, that Gurney's followers had completely abandoned Quakerism. Wilbur, a minister from Rhode Island, was disowned by the New England Yearly Meeting in 1845, and the Philadelphia Yearly Meeting ended its correspondence with New England. In fact, Philadelphia quit communicating with *all* other yearly meetings. It probably seemed safer that way. The Orthodox schism spread as, again, the courts were asked to decide which meetings could keep which property. "On the little island of Nantucket, there were three Friends' Meetinghouses so that Hicksites, Wilburites and Gurneyites could worship" separately, wrote Daisy Newman.[7]

As before, the increased level of evangelical beliefs among Friends found the most favor in the Midwest. Within a few decades, some Friends' meetings featured hymn-singing, a programmed worship service, and paid full-time pastors. The Friends' communities that were formed as the nation expanded westward also tended to be evangelistic. By 1878, the Ohio Yearly Meeting announced: "We repudiate the so-called doctrine of the inner light . . . as dangerous, unsound, and unscriptural,"[8] and some Quakers called for baptism of members in water. In turn, more Friends withdrew from those meetings to reestablish some Quaker traditions, such as the silent meeting.

Joel Bean was a Friend who moved west to escape the conflicts and evangelical influence that were reshaping the Society of Friends. He and his family settled in a small Quaker community outside Los Angeles named for a famous abolitionist Friend—Whittier—but couldn't avoid conflict, after all. Evangelism caught up with Friends in California, too, and Bean and his wife were disowned from their meeting because they wouldn't pay to help support a pastor, just as early Quakers were punished in England for not supporting the established clergy.

The separation of Friends into so many groups eventually "did immense and irreparable harm to all Yearly Meetings and diluted the impact of Friends upon American society," wrote Quaker historians Hugh Barbour and J. William Frost.[9] The Quakers were not unlike other Protestant groups, which had their own series of separations in the nineteenth century. But in the next century, Friends would successfully find ways to communicate with each other and, again, leave an impression on the world that made them seem much larger than their actual membership.

FINDING COMMON GROUND

By the end of the nineteenth century, the Society of Friends was a splintered body whose separate members had little to do with one another. But one holdover remained from their tradition to which they could all relate—service. In the stillness of their quiet meetings, earlier Quakers learned to listen, and the messages they heard led to prison reform, peaceful relationships with Native Americans, freedom for African slaves as well as aid for them after freedom, and humane treatment for the mentally ill. "When a Quaker says, 'I have a concern,' he means that he is so troubled by the suffering of a person or a group of persons . . . that he feels a duty to act on their behalf," wrote Margaret Bacon in *The Quiet Rebels*.[1]

In England, the early Friends had established a Meeting for Sufferings to keep track of injustices against their then-new sect and to pool resources to help Friends facing fines or imprisonment. Later, as Friends became a part of mainstream English and American society, the Meeting for Sufferings was needed more in times of war—Quakers faced hostile neighbors and local governments when they refused to bear arms.

One exception to that was the Civil War, which seemed a more justifiable war to Northern Friends because it could rid the land of slavery. Indiana Quakers sent more than 1,100 men to the Union ranks, almost one fourth of whom died and a small percentage of whom were disowned by their meeting after the war.[2] A Hicksite Quaker colonel from Pennsylvania led what was called the Quaker regiment. Meanwhile, southern Quakers, who refused to defend the Confederate cause, were targets of abuse during the Civil War and had to literally hide from people who sought to punish them for not serving in the Confederate army.

But Friends did not shun the problems caused by war. Quaker women served as nurses to wounded soldiers from both armies, and much material aid was offered to African-Americans who fled to northern states when the Emancipation Proclamation freed all slaves in 1863. Underground Railroad "conductor" Levi Coffin raised more than $87,000 in England for their food, shelter, and clothing. After the war, Friends went south not only to help other Friends who were financially devastated by the conflict, but also to work with freed blacks, opening schools for them throughout the former Confederate states or providing farm and building tools to help them establish homesteads. Baltimore Friends went to North Carolina to try and re-establish public schools there as well as to operate schools for freed blacks, stirring up the wrath of the Ku Klux Klan.

One Friend whose work is mentioned in *The Quiet Rebels* was Cornelia Hancock. When she was twenty years old, Hancock served as a nurse during several Civil War battles. After the war, she went to an island off Charleston, South Carolina, where she used an abandoned church to begin a school for black children, which became the Laing School. After ten years, Hancock returned to Philadelphia, where she helped establish agencies that aided children and families,

After the Civil War, several Quakers built this school in South Carolina for black students.

including a "startlingly modern self-help housing program in a poor section of Philadelphia."[3] In spite of such close interaction between Friends and African-Americans, there were few black Friends meetings formed in the United States, although there were some black members of other meetings.[4]

The suffering of Native Americans in the U.S. also remained a concern for Friends throughout the nineteenth century. Quakers continued to work with eastern Indians on their reservations and, as Friends moved to the Northwest territory, they established Quaker missions for the Native Americans. Out West, after the Civil War, Hicksite Quakers tried to make amends to Indians displaced by the railroad companies by acting on their behalf as government agents. President Ulysses Grant enlisted the Quakers to act as government agents for—and supervisors of—several western reservations. Orthodox Friends worked in Kansas and Hicksites in Nebraska; within a short time, by 1869, schools for Native American children were established and agricultural projects begun.

Eventually, tired of dealing with an unresponsive U.S. government, both Hicksite and Orthodox Quakers worked with Native Americans only as missionaries. Some Indians were converted to the Quaker faith and worshiped in meetinghouses on reservations. Orthodox Quakers tended to emphasize religious conversion in their missionary work, and they eventually went as far north as Alaska to missionize; "convinced" Alaskan natives later formed their own Yearly Meeting. Hicksites focused more on the material needs of those they sought to help, and sometimes they were criticized by Orthodox Quakers for not being spiritual enough in their missionary work.

George Fox first had the idea of operating "a house for them that be distempered."[5] One hundred years later, one of the first large-scale public service projects achieved by colonial Friends in cooperation with other church groups was the Pennsylvania Hospital, established in 1751 to serve poor as well as mentally ill people. It received some financial help from the Pennsylvania state assembly, headed by the Quaker Party, and a separate wing for 100 more mentally ill patients was added in 1796.

*Quakers worked with other groups to build the
Pennsylvania hospital in Philadelphia.*

The Friends Hospital, established in 1817, became the first private institute for the mentally ill in the United States. It had pleasant surroundings and farm work for therapy. There were no chains to restrain patients who, up until 1834, were all Quakers. Like patients in Pennsylvania Hospital, they were treated with compassion and with the assumption that even the mentally ill could heed their Inward Light. Occasionally patients were discharged as cured from the Friends Hospital, though "cures" were considered impossible in that era.

Friends also turned their attention to prisons. Having suffered much in English jails in their early days, it was an issue in which they had a personal interest. When William Penn drew up his Frame of Government for Pennsylvania, and having been jailed in the Tower of London himself, he ordered prisons to provide food and lodging at no cost to prisoners, who would in turn spend their days working in the prison. But after Penn's death, prison conditions in Pennsylvania deteriorated. By the 1700s, American and English prisons didn't differ much from prisons of earlier centuries: children caught stealing were often thrown in with adult murderers, and prisoners had to provide their own food or buy it from the jailers. Some had to beg from passersby from their jail windows.

An organization formed in 1787, the Philadelphia Society for Alleviating the Miseries of the Public Prison (it later gave itself a more manageable name—the Pennsylvania Prison Society), put forth a novel idea: criminals could change their ways. A prison they created was called a *penitentiary*—a place where inmates did penance for their crimes. In New York, Friends worked to have young juvenile prisoners separated from adults.

One experimental prison project that author Margaret Bacon described as a failure was the Eastern Penitentiary, opened in 1829. In order to keep hardened criminals from influencing each other and lesser criminals, all prisoners were kept in isolation day and night—each had a bit of work to do in their cells and a small separate exercise yard. Visits from Friends and prison officials were planned, but, "in practice, the prisoner was virtually isolated from all human contact." A famous English visitor to America, author Charles Dickens, wrote about his travels and described his visit to Eastern Penitentiary. He thought the isolation of the prisoners from human contact "very cruel and severe," as well as "unnatural."[6] That type of imprisonment ended by 1900.

But the Friends continued to seek ways to move beyond the type of imprisonment that had little regard for humanity. Friends didn't neglect women prisoners, either. The work done by Elizabeth Fry, sister of English minister Joseph John Gurney, spurred American women Friends in Philadelphia to create a "halfway house" for women prisoners reentering society.

Another traditional concern of many Friends was the welfare of people in other lands. The earliest Quakers felt the need to bring their spiritual "Truth" to others, and they traveled as far as the Middle East; one Friend went to Rome hoping to convince the Roman Catholic pope, while George Fox wrote to the Chinese emperor about the Quaker faith.

Friends stayed closer to their English or American homes during the 1700s as they worked at regulating their faith; "convincements," or conversions, by the thousands didn't happen anymore as they had in the 1600s, so Friends worked to keep the members they had with strict Disciplines and increasing isolation. But after

America's Civil War, as more and more Quakers adopted an evangelical way of worshiping, a renewed desire to spread their faith occurred, too.

The New England Yearly Meeting sent Eli and Sybil Jones to Palestine, where they helped establish a Quaker school for girls, with a young Palestinian woman as the teacher. Within a few years, various yearly meetings in the Midwest were sending missionary groups to China, India, Mexico, Jamaica, and Alaska. Even the Philadelphia Yearly Meeting, still keeping its distance from other Friends, sent women to Japan to start a girls' school. Several yearly meetings worked together to establish five schools in Cuba.

One of the most fruitful missionary ventures was in East Africa, where the efforts of three young Quakers sent there in 1902 led to what is today a 120,000-strong body of Friends, primarily in Kenya. Nineteenth-century British Friends concerned themselves with civilian war victims in Europe's Crimean War of the 1850s (even visiting the Czar of Russia to attempt to prevent it) and South Africa's Boer War at the end of the century.

By 1900, both the Hicksite and Orthodox Quakers had long talked of re-establishing contact with other Friends' groups; each faction of the Friends felt widely separate from the other two. But one problem they all shared, at least in the eastern United States, was declining membership. The Discipline books among the various groups had ceased to disown members for marrying outside the Quaker faith for fear of losing even more members. Other similarities among the different Quaker groups by the century's end included: temperance (or restricting alcohol consumption), bans on dancing and bearing arms, and equal rights for Native Americans and

By the end of the nineteenth century, many Quakers grew concerned
over declines in membership that left many meetinghouses empty.

African-Americans. Quaker yearly meetings, whatever their affilia-
tion, continued to support charities and missionary work.

Quaker historians Hugh Barbour and J. William Frost wrote in
The Quakers that just as evangelism had begun to influence the
Society of Friends one-hundred years earlier and split it apart, a new
social force would help shape the Quakers and draw them back

together again by 1900: liberalism, a movement away from strict creeds toward an openness to a variety of ideas.

Liberalism in religion made it easier to believe in God and still accept the new theories presented by scientists such as Charles Darwin, who suggested that life on Earth evolved from an earlier state, rather than having appeared suddenly during the Creation depicted in the Bible. Traditionally, Quakerism was adaptable to liberalism, because George Fox never specifically told members what to believe about God, and he considered the individual's relationship with God more important than an outline of beliefs. Quakers had already ended their attempts to remain isolated, and all but a few had given up the plain speech and simple dress.

The Quaker faith was also greatly influenced at this point in its history by Rufus Jones, a Quaker who realized what Friends had in common and overlooked their differences. He was born into a Gurneyite family in South China, Maine, in 1863; the Jones couple who traveled to Palestine in the 1860s to start a school were his aunt and uncle. Jones spent his formative years in a small Quaker community in Maine. He then lived in a slightly larger community at a Quaker boarding school in Rhode Island before receiving his bachelor's and master's degrees from Haverford, a Quaker college near Philadelphia. Although born into the evangelical Quaker branch of Gurneyites, he admitted that "the old way of marrying was lost and forgotten with many other beautiful and precious historical customs" when the Quakers split apart in the mid-1800s.[7]

Rufus Jones became a philosophy teacher at Haverford and was the editor of a Quaker magazine, *American Friend*. He traveled in Europe and met other liberal Friends before he returned to Haverford, where he taught for forty years and wrote more than fifty

Rufus Jones became a central voice for Quakers in the twentieth century.

books, many about Quaker history. As *American Friend* editor, he was able to influence a broad range of Friends. In 1902, he helped gather Friends from New England, the Midwest, and the South into a new unit—the Five Years Meeting—which included Hicksites, Orthodox, and Gurneyites. From that organization grew the Friends United Meeting, today the largest group of Quakers in the country. Capitalizing on the one thing all Friends had in common—their willingness to serve—Jones also helped organize the American Friends Service Committee (AFSC) in 1917, which he directed for thirty years.

Actually, AFSC and its English counterpart, the Friends Service Council of London, served two purposes: they provided troubled spots on the globe with humanitarian aid, and they gave pacifist Friends who didn't want to serve in the twentieth century's two world wars a chance to do something worthwhile and stay out of jail. It was no coincidence that AFSC was organized the same year the United States entered World War I.

The English Friends Service Council had already operated an ambulance service for three years (the war actually began in 1914) when AFSC joined it in France to help war victims. Their jobs included hospital and orphanage work, building temporary housing, and helping farmers plant and harvest food, as well as the distribution of food, clothing, and household items to those in need. Their ranks swelled to 600 men and women and included other pacifist church members such as Mennonites and Brethren; American Friends' groups raised almost half of the $2 million needed for the relief work.

When the war ended in November 1918, the defeated Germans also faced severe hardship, and English Friends immediately went there to help. One year later, U.S. government official and Quaker Herbert Hoover (who would be elected president in 1928) asked AFSC to oversee larger-scale relief efforts in Germany, where people were starving. By February 1920, American Friends were in Berlin, and by summer more than 600,000 German children and pregnant and nursing mothers were given one meal a day in hundreds of German communities; in the next year, it became 1 million children each day. The U.S. government provided the food, the German government provided the transportation and thousands of volunteers, and 28 AFSC representatives ran the program.[8] The year 1921 was

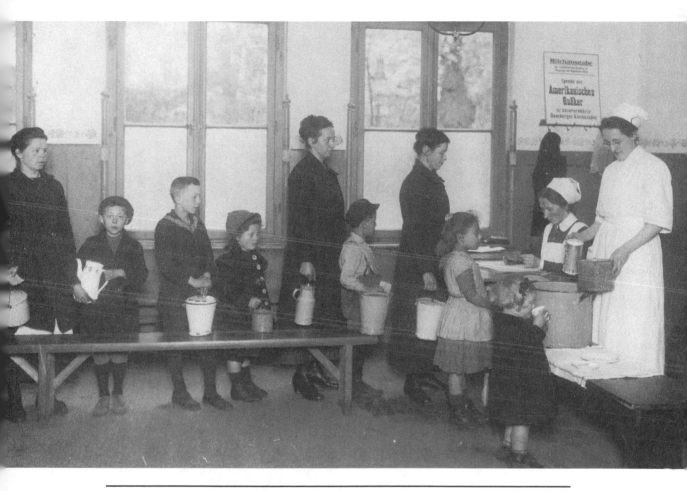

*After World War I, Quakers traveled to Germany
and distributed food to hungry children.*

very busy: Friends' Service Committee representatives also went to
Russia to work with famine victims.

Between the world wars, AFSC set up a series of offices in several European cities. Peace and prosperity were scarce between the
stormy wars: a major economic depression affected Europe and the

The Quakers devoted enormous amounts of energy to alleviate the destruction and pain caused by World War II.

United States; Spain, which remained neutral during the world wars, endured a civil war in the 1930s; and Germany's Nazi party began causing tremors of troubles to come later in the 1930s.

The Friends Service Committees came to the aid of civilians on both sides of the Spanish conflict. The Jewish situation in Germany seemed serious enough that, in 1938, three American Quakers, including Rufus Jones, sailed to Europe, hoping to meet with Adolf Hitler's staff and win a promise of better treatment of Germany's Jewish citizens. Though they never gained access to any "higher-ups" on Hitler's staff and instead spoke with members of the Nazi secret police, there was a temporary increase of immigration visas granted to German Jews after the Quakers' visit. Within a year, Germany invaded Poland and World War II began, and the British and American Service Committees worked at peak capacity with refugees for the next several years. A famine in India became a concern of the committees, and AFSC also put much effort into situations occurring in the United States, such as hardship to families of coal miners in West Virginia during the Depression, and the internment of Japanese Americans during World War II. When the service committees won the Nobel Peace Prize in 1947, the prize money was used to buy medicine for children suffering from tuberculosis in the Soviet Union.

In spite of the service they offered, Quaker conscientious objectors (or C.O.'s, the term for those who feel they cannot bear arms in wartime) often were held in contempt by patriotic Americans and British. Anger against the German aggressors was feverish in both countries, especially during the First World War. C.O.s not only had to perform service for no pay, but sometimes had

In 1947, the Friends service committees won the Nobel peace prize.

to pay for their keep. One New York minister called Quaker pacifism "unscriptural," because he said Jesus didn't require it of his followers. But, said a Friend in response: "The Quaker opposition to
war arises . . . not from fear of a physical death, but from a concep-
tion of how the world is to be remade."[9]

Not all Quakers have agreed on pacifism, note Barbour and
Frost in *The Quakers*. Quietists and Evangelicals alike have support-

ed war efforts, from the American Revolution up through World War II. During the Vietnam War in the 1960s and 1970s, many Quakers were outraged when independently acting Friends arranged to have medicine delivered to North Vietnam.

During the Vietnam War, Quaker groups shipped needed supplies to devastated areas in Southeast Asia.

But in spite of these internal tensions, the wars of the twentieth century were a catalyst, occurring amid a general desire for unity, in bringing Friends back together. Today, the various branches of Friends coexist, not always relating to one another very well, but valuing their common and honorable heritage enough to at least accept one another. As with all worthwhile endeavors, the Friends still face challenges, as some of their current members discuss in the next chapter.

QUAKERS TODAY

7

*E*astern Hills Friends Meeting just outside Cincinnati, Ohio, is
a typical unprogrammed American Friends meeting in many
ways. Its newer, one-story meetinghouse is simple, looking
somewhat like a ranch-style house on the outside and devoid of any
decoration inside. And its location is in a mostly white American
middle/upper-class suburb of the city.

Inside, theater-type chairs arranged in a square provide comfortable seating for sixty people, half of which might be filled for ten
o'clock Meeting on any Sunday morning. Officially, forty-four
members are registered in this Meeting. Large windows fill the room
with natural light; a few small posters featuring quotes from George
Fox, hung in no particular pattern, break up the wall's dark panel-
ing. Meeting begins with a hymn, accompanied by a member at the
piano, and then the silence commences.

One winter day's meeting is attended by about a dozen young
children, who are not as still in their seats as their parents, but are

quiet nonetheless. After 10 or 15 minutes, three adults lead the children to adjoining rooms for their religious education. The one teenager at the meeting has a class by himself with his teacher. Amid muffled sounds of children talking and laughing, the silence of the meeting continues until someone feels led to speak.

One young woman speaks of the military-type toy airplane her son wanted to bring to meeting, and she and her husband decided that this toy wouldn't be appropriate for a Quaker gathering. That, however, leads her to think about the diversity among Quakers—those who are pacifists and those who find nothing wrong with defending one's country, for example. "Those kinds of differences can strengthen our religion," she says, and in the end no one is excluded.

After a few more minutes a man speaks up. He describes the subtle solar wind that reaches Earth, and which is often difficult to detect. He compared it to God's spirit, which can be just as easy to ignore—or we can watch for it, and set our life's course by it. Again, a few minutes pass and a last speaker expresses her gratitude "for the grace of a new day" and the opportunity to put bad decisions and choices into the past and begin the day anew.

The meeting ends at eleven o'clock, as children rejoin their parents in the main room. After a few minutes of socializing, most of the day's attendants leave, while a few stay behind for their weekly look at the Bible. The Bible study is something new they are trying; the meeting is whatever they make it.

Across town, in another suburb, Cincinnati Friends Meeting is getting its Sunday meeting underway. Though pastor-led, their pastor, Ed Balogh, jokes that his meetings are only "semi-programmed." Hymns are sung from a Christian hymnbook but are not planned in advance. Members choose them spontaneously, much as they might feel led to speak. Balogh gives a sermon he's prepared, and the rest of the meeting is the traditional Quaker silence.

This meeting was established in 1811 by North Carolinians who came to Cincinnati after first buying as many slaves as possible in order to free them in the new state of Ohio. Their first meeting-house was a Presbyterian log cabin in what is now downtown Cincinnati. Today, the meeting is in its fourth building, each one getting farther from the city. About thirty years old, the current meeting-house was designed to be simple and un-church-like. Inside, it's patterned after an old English Quaker meetinghouse.

Cincinnati Friends and Eastern Hills monthly meetings are both affiliated with Friends United Meeting, which includes unprogrammed as well as programmed meetings. Eastern Hills also belongs to Friends General Conference, which is based in Philadelphia and made up of unprogrammed meetings. Other Quaker groups include Evangelical Friends Alliance and, perhaps its opposite, the smaller Conservative Friends, among whom use of "thee" and "thou" are not uncommon.

Not surprisingly, with their broad range of practices and beliefs, Friends have veered toward further divisions in the last thirty years. Evangelical Friends Alliance might have formed into a separate Quaker church, but they chose to remain under the broader umbrella of Friends during a special meeting called in 1970. More recently, the "Richmond Declaration," issued by Indiana Yearly Meeting in 1987 and containing strict definitions of Christian beliefs, threatened to split the Friends United Meeting down liberal and conservative lines, but, again, unity was chosen over requiring specific beliefs. A joint statement was issued that "Friends United Meeting is an organization that, amid the diverse body that is the Society of Friends today, comes together to witness and work based on a common commitment to Jesus Christ."[1]

Diversity among American Friends also includes support—or lack of it—for the American Friends Service Committee, which some Friends believe has over the years increasingly lent its aid to "radical and violent liberation movements across the world, especially in the Middle East and southern Africa," as Quaker author Larry Ingle wrote in a recent magazine article.[2] Many of the country's largest yearly meetings no longer have any ties to the AFSC. The Service Committee has also been criticized for the small number of Quakers on its staff. Abortion and homosexuality are other issues that divide Friends.

While religious diversity abounds among Friends, its members admit that American Friends are largely white, middle-class, educated suburban dwellers. And some Quakers worry about the faith's membership numbers. The minimum age for applying for membership to a meeting is about eighteen. Eastern Hills meeting members said that only a small percentage of children raised in the Quaker faith remain with it as adults, because "we do not tell them all the time what to believe." Their own unprogrammed meeting is not aggressive in seeking out new members. Ed Balogh said that in smaller communities, Quaker families often stay with a meeting for generations, something not as easily accomplished in urban areas. "We don't do a good job" of keeping children within the faith as adults, said Neil Snarr, who presides as clerk over the Wilmington Yearly Meeting in southwestern Ohio.

One potential future Friend is Nissen Lund, a high school sophomore in Cincinnati. He attends a large, urban, college

Although there is great religious diversity among Quakers, they still tend to be like these Quakers photographed in the 1920s or 1930s: white and upper middle class. Today, Quakers hope to expand their faith to different groups in American society.

preparatory high school and finds that his Quaker upbringing affects who he is today. "Being a Quaker, I find I have different values than my peers," he says. He has taken to heart, for example, the Quaker tradition of living simply. "I'm not interested in clothes or style."

"I appreciate my faith quite a bit. It's very open, and doesn't condemn other religions for necessarily being wrong," he says. Unlike many Quaker youths of two-hundred years ago who were sheltered in their faith by attending Quaker schools, Nissen knows few other Friends his own age. One of his closest friends from school is a Roman Catholic. "I don't have many friends I can relate to, religiously." He can't claim he will remain a Quaker, though, in spite of his appreciation of it.

But some yearly meetings are growing, including that of Baltimore, which has added new monthly meetings. Karen Treber is one Friend from the Baltimore Yearly Meeting who became "convinced" in her college years; she and her husband, David, who grew up in the Quaker faith, live in suburban Washington, D.C., with their two young children.

Karen became a Quaker while attending Bryn Mawr, a women's college established by Quakers near Philadelphia. Out of curiosity, she attended a Quaker meeting at nearby Haverford and was drawn to the unprogrammed meeting's approach to God. Out of college and working in Washington, D.C., she met her husband at the Quaker meeting they both attended. He grew up in central Indiana, attending a Quaker meeting that calls itself a church, and which has a pastor, an altar, and an organ. It has a silent period lasting several minutes, but members often use that time to pray aloud for special intentions.

Their Langley Hill Meeting in MacLean, Virginia, is unprogrammed. The Trebers chose to attend it because it has an abundance of young children and a religious education program for them. The meeting bought an old Protestant church in MacLean; it has a steeple, but members removed the stained-glass window and rearranged the wooden pews into a square.

When the Trebers were married, they wrote a letter expressing their desire to do so "under the care of the meeting," which then

*At this modern Quaker meeting, a young couple
sits in the center and prepares for marriage.*

assumes a responsibility to help them along in their married life when needed. For unprogrammed Friends, a member of the meeting receives a certificate from the state government allowing them to verify weddings. The Trebers bent the rules a bit on Quaker simplicity for their wedding: Karen wore a full-length gown and veil, David wore a tuxedo, and each had an attendant. They said their vows to each other, and then the meeting progressed as usual. Afterward, everyone from the meeting signed their wedding certificate, which now hangs in their home.

Karen is a lawyer and serves on the Friends Committee for National Legislation, a lobbying committee with an office in Washington, D.C. Lately, the FCNL has been concerned with the United States' decreased participation in the United Nations and has urged federal lawmakers to balance the budget by cutting military spending rather than funds for social programs.

Both the monthly meeting in Virginia that the Trebers now attend and the Quaker church where David worshiped as a child are part of Friends United Meeting, a perfect example of the broad form of worship that the Quaker faith embraces. Like the members of the Eastern Hills Friends Meeting in Ohio, Karen would like to see more economic and ethnic diversity among Friends in America.

Although there is a large number of Friends in Africa, minority-member Friends are few and far between in the English-speaking countries. The differences of "cultural styles of worship" between the quiet white Quakers and the emotional, enthusiastic worship associated with African-Americans is usually the reason given when Friends ask themselves about their lack of minority members, said Daniel Smith-Christopher, a Quaker and a theology associate professor at

Loyola–Marymount University in Los Angeles. But the growing body of evangelistic Quakers shouldn't have that problem, he said.

"It is a concern," said Neil Snarr, who worries that Quakers, who now enjoy middle- to upper-class lifestyles, have become "too successful, too comfortable" to reach out as they once did. Not far from his home in Wilmington, Ohio, is the small town of Harveysburg, where the first school for freed blacks was established in Ohio by Friends early in the last century. That old school building is still standing, but the town's Friends meeting is long gone.

Snarr said that the number of unprogrammed meetings are growing, too, in America. Perhaps, as those Friends heed the inner voice that inspired George Fox, their "concerns" will outweigh their comfort.

SOURCE NOTES

Chapter 2

1. H. Larry Ingle, *First Among Friends: George Fox and the Creation of Quakerism* (Oxford University Press, 1994), p. 44.
2. Ingle, p. 59.
3. Ingle, p. 76.
4. Hugh Barbour & J. William Frost, *The Quakers* (Greenwood Press, New York, 1988), p. 29.
5. Barbour & Frost, p. 39.
6. Rufus M. Jones, *Faith and Practice of the Quakers* (George H. Doran & Co., New York, 1927), p. 35.
7. Jones, p. 43.

Chapter 3

1. Daisy Newman, *Procession of Friends: Quakers in America* (Doubleday & Co., Garden City, N.Y., 1972), p. 7.
2. Newman, p. 10.

3. Newman, p. 32.

4 Hugh Barbour & William J. Frost, *The Quakers* (Greenwood Press, New York, 1988), p. 52.

5. Barbour & Frost, p. 56.

6. Barbour & Frost, p. 61.

7. Richard Dunn & Mary Maples Dunn, "World of William Penn," (University of Pennsylvania Press, Philadelphia, 1986), p. 45.

8. Barbour & Frost, p. 75.

9. Barbour & Frost, p. 109.

10. Barbour & Frost, p. 100.

Chapter 4

1. Hugh Barbour & William J. Frost, *The Quakers* (Greenwood Press, New York, 1988), p. 132.

2. Daisy Newman, *Procession of Friends: Quakers in America* (Doubleday & Co., Garden City, N.Y., 1972), p. 70.

3. Margaret H. Bacon, *The Quiet Rebels: The Story of the Quakers in America* (Basic Books, Inc., New York, 1969), p. 111.

4. Bacon, p. 115.

Chapter 5

1. Margaret H. Bacon, *The Quiet Rebels: The Story of the Quakers in America* (Basic Books, Inc., New York, 1969), p. 75.

2. Daisy Newman, *Procession of Friends: Quakers in America* (Doubleday & Co., Garden City, N.Y., 1972), p. 89.

3. Bacon, p. 86.

4. Ibid.

5. Bacon, p. 88.

6. Hugh Barbour & William J. Frost, *The Quakers* (Greenwood Press, New York, 1988), p. 179.
7. Newman, p. 110.
8. Newman, p. 120.
9. Barbour & Frost, p. 181.

Chapter 6

1. Margaret H. Bacon, *The Quiet Rebels: The Story of the Quakers in America* (Basic Books, Inc., New York, 1969), p. 122.
2. Hugh Barbour & William J. Frost, *The Quakers* (Greenwood Press, New York, 1988), p. 197.
3. Bacon, p. 120–121.
4. Barbour & Frost, p. 198.
5. Bacon, p. 139.
6. Bacon, p. 134.
7. Daisy Newman, *Procession of Friends: Quakers in America* (Doubleday & Co., Garden City, N.Y., 1972), p. 124.
8. Barbour & Frost, p. 253.
9. Newman, p. 134.

Chapter 7

1. *Christian Century* (September 9–16, 1987), p. 742.
2. *Christian Century* (April 19, 1995), p. 412.

FOR FURTHER READING

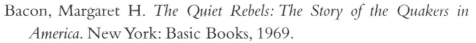

Bacon, Margaret H. *The Quiet Rebels: The Story of the Quakers in America*. New York: Basic Books, 1969.

Barbour, Hugh, and J. William Frost. *The Quakers*. New York: Greenwood Press, 1988.

Ingle, H. Larry. *First Among Friends: George Fox and the Creation of Quakerism*. New York: Oxford University Press, 1994.

Jones, Rufus M. *Faith and Practice of the Quakers*. New York: George H. Doran & Co., 1927.

Newman, Daisy. *Procession of Friends: Quakers in America*. New York: Doubleday & Co., 1972.

INTERNET SITES

Due to the changeable nature of the Internet, sites appear and disappear very quickly. Internet addresses must be entered with capital and lowercase letters exactly as they appear.

The Yahoo directory of the World Wide Web is an excellent place to find Internet sites on any topic. The directory is located at:

http://www.yahoo.com

George Fox wrote an autobiography detailing his life experiences and his philosophy on religion. The entire text is available at:

http://www.mindspring.com/~kwattles/gfox/title.html

The city of Philadelphia was the heart of Quaker society during the colonial period. To take a virtual tour of the city's historic sites, visit:

http://www.libertynet.org/iha/

INDEX

ABOUT THE AUTHOR

Jean Kinney Williams grew up in Ohio and lives there now with her husband and four children. She studied journalism in college and, in addition to writing, enjoys reading, volunteering at church, and spending time with her family. She is the author of the Franklin Watts First Book *Matthew Hensen: Polar Adventurer* (1994) and of four other American Religious Experience books, *The Amish* (1996), *The Christian Scientists* (1997), *The Mormons* (1996), and *The Shakers* (1997).